OUR BILL OF RIGHTS

POWERS OF THE PEOPLE

A LOOK AT THE NINTH AND TENTH AMENDMENTS

GERALDINE P. LYMAN

PowerKiDS
press.

NEW YORK

Published in 2019 by The Rosen Publishing Group, Inc.
29 East 21st Street, New York, NY 10010

Editor: Sharon Gleason
Book Design: Rachel Rising

Photo Credits: Cover Monkey Business Images/Shutterstock.com; Cover, pp. 1, 3, 4, 6, 7, 8, 9, 10, 11, 12, 13, 14, 15, 16, 17, 18 ,19, 20, 22, 23, 24, 26, 27, 28, 29, 30, 31, 32 (background) Mad Dog/Shutterstock.com; Cover, pp. 1, 3, 4, 6, 7, 8, 9, 10, 11, 12, 13, 14, 15, 16, 17, 18 ,19, 20, 22, 23, 24, 26, 27, 28, 29, 30, 31, 32 (background) Flas100/Shutterstock.com; p. 5 Alex Wong/Staff/Getty Images News/Getty Images; pp. 7, 13 Courtesy of The Library of Congress; p. 7 (Hamilton) https://commons.wikimedia.org/wiki/File:Alexander_Hamilton_portrait_by_John_Trumbull_1806.jpg; p. 7 (background) monofaction/Shutterstock.com; pp. 8, 14, 16, 20, 26 (arrow) Forest Foxy/Shutterstock.com; p. 9 Sean Pavone/Shutterstock.com; p. 11 NaughtyNut/Shutterstock.com; p. 15 Everett-Art/Shutterstock.com; p. 17 Syda Productions/Shutterstock.com; p. 18 Lee Lockwood/The LIFE Images Collection/Getty Images; p. 19 Alfred Eisenstaedt/The LIFE Picture Collection/Getty Images;p. 21 Keith Homan/Shutterstock.com; p. 23 SuperStock/Getty Images; p. 25 Cameron Whitman/Shutterstock.com; p. 27 Shel Hershorn- HA/Inactive/Contributor/Archive Photos/Getty Images; p. 28 fg76/Shutterstock.com; p. 29 Rena Schild/Shutterstock.com; p. 30 Vlue/Shutterstock.com.

Library of Congress Cataloging-in-Publication Data

Names: Lyman, Geraldine P., author.
Title: Powers of the people : a look at the Ninth and Tenth Amendments /
   Geraldine P. Lyman.
Description: New York : PowerKids Press, [2019] | Series: Our Bill of Rights
   | Includes index.
Identifiers: LCCN 2018025105| ISBN 9781538343142 (library bound) | ISBN
   9781538343128 (pbk.) | ISBN 9781538343135 (6 pack)
Subjects: LCSH: United States. Constitution 9th Amendment--Juvenile
   literature. | United States. Constitution 10th Amendment--Juvenile
   literature. | Constituent power--United States--Juvenile literature. |
   Federal government--United States--Juvenile literature. | States' rights
   (American politics)--Juvenile literature. | Civil rights--United
   States--Juvenile literature.
Classification: LCC KF4557 .L96 2019 | DDC 342.73/042--dc23
LC record available at https://lccn.loc.gov/2018025105

Manufactured in the United States of America

CPSIA Compliance Information: Batch #CWPK19 For further information contact Rosen Publishing, New York, New York at 1-800-237-9932.

CONTENTS

THE PAPERS THAT GUIDE OUR COUNTRY

The United States government is guided by several important **documents**. These documents were written during the American Revolution and the country's early years. The Constitution, written in 1787, includes rules that determine the organization of the nation. The Constitution divides the government into three branches: legislative (Congress), judicial (federal courts), and executive (president). It also includes rights promised to every citizen.

The Bill of Rights includes some of the most important rules and rights. It includes 10 amendments, or changes, to the Constitution that protect the individual rights of American citizens. It was written by James Madison, ratified, or approved, by the states, and added to the Constitution in 1791.

KNOW YOUR RIGHTS!

July 4 is the day we celebrate the founding of the United States. It marks the day the Declaration of Independence was finalized in 1776. However, it wasn't signed by the Founding Fathers until August 2, 1776. The Constitution was signed 11 years later, on September 17, 1787.

The Declaration of Independence, the Constitution, and the Bill of Rights are housed at the National Archives in Washington, D.C.

FEDERALISTS AND ANTI-FEDERALISTS

When the country was new, there were a lot of **debates** about what should be included in the Constitution. Some people wanted a very strong federal government that would be able to make decisions for the whole country. These people were called the Federalists. Alexander Hamilton, John Jay, and James Madison were Federalists who wrote their opinions in a series of letters sometimes called "the Federalist Papers."

Other people preferred the idea of strong state governments, with the federal government having limited powers. These people were called the anti-Federalists. Anti-Federalists such as Patrick Henry, George Mason, and Richard Henry Lee were suspicious of the government. After fighting against Great Britain in the American Revolution, the anti-Federalists wanted little government **involvement** in their lives. They feared a big national government could take away their freedom and individual rights.

THE FEDERALIST PAPERS

Sometimes when people want to express a political opinion, they'll write a letter to a newspaper, hoping it'll get published. This is exactly what Hamilton, Jay, and Madison did in the 1780s. Over several years, they wrote 85 letters in support of ratifying the Constitution. They submitted these letters under the pseudonym, or chosen name, "Publius." In 1788, the letters were collected and published as a book called *The Federalist*.

Alexander Hamilton wrote most of the letters contained in *The Federalist*.

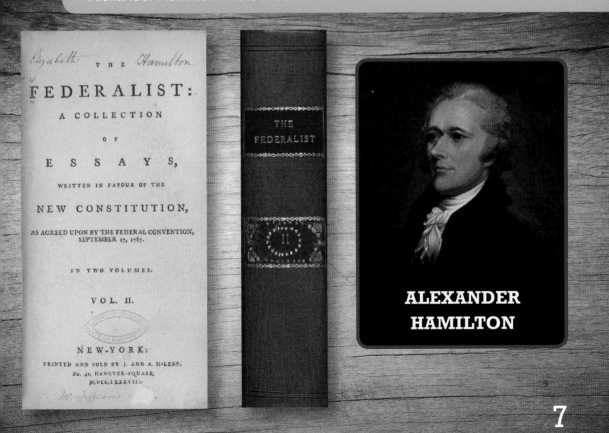

THE

FEDERALIST:

A COLLECTION

OF

E S S A Y S,

WRITTEN IN FAVOUR OF THE

NEW CONSTITUTION,

AS AGREED UPON BY THE FEDERAL CONVENTION,
SEPTEMBER 17, 1787.

IN TWO VOLUMES.

VOL. II.

NEW-YORK:

PRINTED AND SOLD BY J. AND A. M'LEAN,
No. 41, HANOVER-SQUARE,
M,DCC,LXXXVIII.

THE
FEDERALIST

II

**ALEXANDER
HAMILTON**

WAS THE CONSTITUTION ENOUGH?

Before the Constitution was ratified, the United States followed a set of rules called the Articles of Confederation. It established a very weak central government and allowed for the states to mostly make their own decisions, except when dealing with other nations. However, this early constitution was difficult to enforce. Leaders soon decided a stronger government was necessary. So, they created the Constitution.

The U.S. Constitution details the powers of the federal government. Federalists considered this to be all the country needed. Anti-Federalists, worried about creating a government that was too powerful and would take away individual rights, thought the Constitution wasn't enough. Before approving the Constitution, they called for changes to list the protected rights citizens and states would have. These amendments became known as the Bill of Rights.

The Constitutional Convention was held at the Pennsylvania State House, now known as Independence Hall, in Philadelphia.

THE ARTICLES OF CONFEDERATION

Once the states declared their independence from Great Britain, they needed new rules to establish how government would work. The first constitution was called the Articles of Confederation. Several politicians wrote early **versions** of it, but John Dickinson's version became the basis for the final document. It took several years, and many changes, before all the states ratified it. Maryland was the last to do so, in 1781.

ADDING A BILL OF RIGHTS

During the Constitutional Convention, Founding Father George Mason said that he wished the Constitution included a Bill of Rights. Other anti-Federalists agreed. Many decided that they wouldn't move forward without such changes.

James Madison was a Federalist who supported the Constitution. However, he knew the Constitution needed anti-Federalists' support. He promised to create a series of amendments to satisfy anti-Federalists and reviewed many suggestions from the states. His final work was inspired by many governments' statements of rights. Virginia's Declaration of Rights, which was written by Mason, was a big influence. So was the Magna Carta, which limited the powers of British royalty when it was signed in 1215.

KNOW YOUR RIGHTS!

The Magna Carta is an important historical document. Nobles in England wrote it to help stop King John's mistreatment of his people. For the framers, or creators, of the Constitution, the Magna Carta was a model of how people can stand up to **oppressive** leadership.

George Mason refused to sign the Constitution because it didn't include a Bill of Rights or end the slave trade.

Madison drafted a list of amendments. After some changes, the House of Representatives and the Senate approved many of them. Eventually, 10 amendments were ratified by the states and became the Bill of Rights.

THE NINTH AND TENTH AMENDMENTS

The Bill of Rights has 10 amendments. The Ninth and Tenth Amendments aren't talked about as much as the First, Second, or even the Eighth Amendment. The Ninth and Tenth Amendments don't specify certain rights of the people, unlike many of the other amendments. Instead, they deal with the strength of the federal government and act as final checks to make sure that future federal leaders won't have too much power or take away rights.

By ensuring some final limits on the federal government, these two amendments played a key role, or part, in the debate between the Federalists and the anti-Federalists. They reassured those who were worried about the federal government becoming too powerful. They also made sure the Bill of Rights couldn't be used to take away rights that weren't listed in it.

Patrick Henry opposed the Constitution because he thought it would make the federal government too powerful.

KNOW YOUR RIGHTS!

Patrick Henry was an important Founding Father who was an anti–Federalist. For many years, he was opposed to the British government and its taxes. He's well known for the famous speech in which he said, "Give me liberty or give me death!"

RETAINED BY THE PEOPLE

"The **enumeration** in the Constitution, of certain rights, shall not be **construed** to deny or **disparage** others retained by the people."

Why did the Founding Fathers think the Ninth Amendment was necessary? Let's take a closer look.

At the time, some Founding Fathers were worried that, if they created a list of rights, these rights might be considered the only rights people had. The government would have far too much power! This is an argument that those against a bill of rights brought up. Even James Madison considered it a problem. So, he wrote what became the Ninth Amendment. In simpler words, the amendment means that just because a right isn't listed in the Constitution or Bill of Rights, it doesn't mean that people don't have that right.

James Madison didn't believe a Bill of Rights was necessary, but he knew it was needed to get states to ratify the Constitution.

JAMES MADISON

James Madison was born in Virginia in 1751. A Founding Father and a Federalist, he wrote the first versions of both the U.S. Constitution and the Bill of Rights, earning him the title "Father of the Constitution." With Thomas Jefferson, he later founded the Democratic-Republican Party. From 1801 to 1809, he served as the secretary of state under President Jefferson, and from 1809 to 1817, he served as the fourth president of the United States.

THE RIGHT TO PRIVACY?

Many people over the years have disagreed about the Ninth Amendment. Courts don't often refer to it. Its language may seem vague. In part, this may have been on purpose—if the Bill of Rights could name every right that people have, we wouldn't need the Ninth Amendment!

Because the Ninth Amendment is so broad, people often have different opinions about what it means. Some people think it refers to rights given by state laws. Others say it refers to the collective rights of the people, or the rights people have as a group. Yet others say it refers to certain natural rights everyone should have. One such right, some say, is privacy. This right isn't specifically listed in the Constitution.

As online privacy becomes an important issue in today's society, the Ninth Amendment may become an important part of deciding what the government can and can't **monitor**.

ORIGINALISTS

The Constitution is a document that was designed to stay **relevant** over a long period of time. However, many people have different interpretations of it. Originalists are people who believe that the meaning of the U.S. Constitution should be considered exactly as it was stated when the Constitution was first ratified.

GRISWOLD V. CONNECTICUT

In 1965, the case of *Griswold v. Connecticut* brought some attention to the Ninth Amendment. Birth control, or ways to avoid having babies, was illegal in Connecticut. Estelle Griswold was arrested and fined for helping people get birth control. After several appeals, her case went to the Supreme Court.

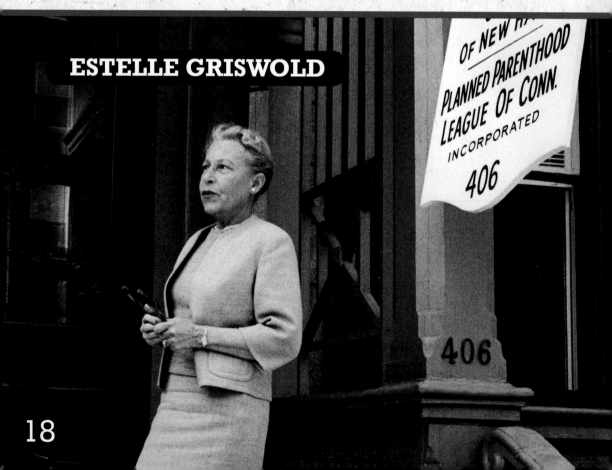

ESTELLE GRISWOLD

These nine justices made up the Supreme Court that ruled on *Griswold v. Connecticut*: Thomas Clark, Hugo Black, Earl Warren, William Douglas, John Harlan, Byron White, William Brennan, Potter Stewart, and Arthur Goldberg. Black and Stewart disagreed with the decision.

The Supreme Court looked at multiple amendments when it considered the case. Eventually, the court decided that people had rights to "zones of privacy," within which the government couldn't interfere, and that the law should be struck down. The justices looked at the meanings of the First, Third, Fourth, and Fifth Amendments, all of which covered parts of a right to privacy. Finally, they said that, according to the Ninth Amendment, privacy was a right not mentioned but implied by the Constitution.

THE POWERS NOT DELEGATED

The Tenth Amendment reads: "The powers not delegated to the United States by the Constitution, nor **prohibited** by it to the States, are reserved to the States **respectively**, or to the people."

This was a way to assure anti-Federalists that states still held a lot of governmental power. It assures that powers that aren't given to the federal government in the Constitution are given to the states or the people. The Bill of Rights doesn't change this. This amendment means that states create and have their own laws as long as they don't interfere with those of the federal government. For example, relationships between any part of the United States and other countries are specifically for the federal government to oversee.

Though there are now 27 amendments in the Constitution, the Bill of Rights just includes the first 10.

CAREFUL WORDING

The Tenth Amendment is based on a part of the Articles of Confederation. The original part of the Articles of Confederation reads: "Each state retains its sovereignty, freedom, and independence, and every power, **jurisdiction**, and right, which is not by this confederation expressly delegated to the United States, in Congress assembled."

This isn't quite the same as the Tenth Amendment. For one thing, the Articles of Confederation use the word "expressly." This meant that the federal government's only powers were written out in the Articles of Confederation. Madison was determined that "expressly" wouldn't be included in this amendment to the Constitution. He knew the Constitution couldn't list every single implied power of the federal government, and he wanted to make the Constitution flexible, or able to adjust to new laws and situations.

KNOW YOUR RIGHTS!

The U.S. Constitution gives the federal government the implied powers "necessary and proper" for using its specific powers.

The Constitutional Convention was held in 1787 to revise, or improve, the Articles of Confederation.

IS THE TENTH AMENDMENT NECESSARY?

Today, the Tenth Amendment can be a hotly debated topic. People disagree about how big a part the federal government should play in their everyday lives and how much power it should have.

Courts have had different opinions. In 1931, the Supreme Court ruled on the case *United States v. Sprague*. Justice Owen Roberts, who gave the final opinion, or decision, of the Supreme Court, wrote: "The Tenth Amendment was intended to confirm the understanding of the people. . . . It added nothing to the instrument as originally ratified." This means that he and the rest of the justices who agreed with the opinion believed that the Tenth Amendment didn't add anything new to the Constitution. It's just there to make things clear.

KNOW YOUR RIGHTS!

The Supreme Court has nine justices. One of the powers of the court is deciding whether or not laws are constitutional. This power is called judicial review.

The Supreme Court building is located in Washington, D.C.

"STATES' RIGHTS" AND DISCRIMINATION

The Tenth Amendment has been interpreted and reinterpreted in many ways. In the years leading up to the Civil War, the Tenth Amendment was applied to the issue of slavery. Some called it a state's right and some called the decisions about slavery an implied right of the federal government.

In 1948, a group of Southerners formed the States' Rights Democratic Party. Also known as the Dixiecrats, the party interpreted the Tenth Amendment as expressly limiting the federal government. They focused on challenging federal powers. Specifically, the party disagreed with federal laws aimed at **desegregation**. "States' rights" became a phrase associated with **discrimination** against African Americans and opposition to the growing civil rights movement. After the 1954 *Brown v. Board of Education* Supreme Court decision, which desegregated schools, states' rights rallies occurred in some states.

Brigadier General Henry V. Graham approaches Governor George Wallace to say that federal National Guard troops have entered the University of Alabama campus to enforce desegregation.

DESEGREGATING THE UNIVERSITY OF ALABAMA

In one of the clearest clashes of state and federal government power in the 20th century, Governor George Wallace of Alabama ignored a federal order to desegregate the University of Alabama, blocking African American students from registering for class. President John F. Kennedy sent the Alabama National Guard to force Wallace to surrender. After Wallace stepped aside, Vivian Malone and James Hood became the first African American students to enter the school and register for classes.

DEFENDING THE TENTH

The Tenth Amendment has many supporters. Recently, the "Tenther" movement has been urging state governments to push for their rights. People who belong to this movement believe that the federal government has been playing too much of a role in the day-to-day life of American citizens.

On June 26, 2015, a Supreme Court decision made same-sex marriage legal in all 50 states. The Tenther movement believes that only states should decide laws regarding marriage.

In 2009, 37 states introduced resolutions that push the idea of states' rights. Though symbolic, these resolutions show that some state governments feel the need to promote the rights they say the Tenth Amendment gives them.

Not everyone agrees with the movement. Some have spoken out against the goals of the Tenthers, saying that the movement misinterprets the Constitution.

STRONG AND IN CHECK

The Constitution is an old document, but the arguments of the Federalists and anti-Federalists still apply today. Maybe it's not always obvious, but the Ninth and Tenth Amendments have affected your life, as they've affected the lives of all who live in the United States.

Congress carefully created the Ninth and Tenth Amendments and made sure every word mattered. Members worked to make sure that these final amendments of the Bill of Rights kept the Constitution flexible enough to cover a variety of situations and satisfy those with different views. They are important building blocks that keep the balance of power between the people, the states, and the federal government in check.

GLOSSARY

construe: To understand something in a particular way.

debate: A discussion in which people express different opinions, or to discuss different opinions about something.

desegregation: Ending the practice of keeping people of different groups separate.

discrimination: Different—usually unfair—treatment based on factors such as a person's race, age, religion, or gender.

disparage: To make lower in importance, or to speak about someone in an unfavorable way.

document: A formal piece of writing.

enumeration: The act of making a numbered list.

involvement: The act or state of being involved, or being a part of something.

jurisdiction: The power to make decisions about laws.

monitor: To observe and check the progress of something.

oppressive: Unjustly harsh or severe.

prohibit: To order or prevent someone from doing something.

relevant: Important to what's happening at the time.

respectively: In the order given.

version: A form of something that is different from the ones that came before it.

INDEX

WEBSITES

Due to the changing nature of Internet links, PowerKids Press has developed an online list of
websites related to the subject of this book. This site is updated regularly. Please use this link to
access the list: www.powerkidslinks.com/obor/ninthtenth